# Helen Boyles

# Catching Light

**Indigo Dreams Publishing**

First Edition: Catching Light
First published in Great Britain in 2016 by:
Indigo Dreams Publishing Ltd
24 Forest Houses
Halwill
Beaworthy
EX21 5UU
www.indigodreams.co.uk

ISBN 978-1-910834-05-3

British Library Cataloguing in Publication Data. A CIP record for this book can be obtained from the British Library.

Designed and typeset in Palatino Linotype by Indigo Dreams.
Cover design and photo by Ronnie Goodyer at Indigo Dreams

Printed and bound in Great Britain by 4edge Ltd.

Papers used by Indigo Dreams are recyclable products made from wood grown in sustainable forests following the guidance of the Forest Stewardship Council.

*To my parents*

# Acknowledgements

I would like to thank my poetry-loving parents for their constant encouragement and belief in me as a writer, the like-minded Devon-based poetic community of Moor Poets with their stimulating  workshops and opportunity for creative sharing, and local groups of poetry enthusiasts who have provided a welcome platform on which to share my poetry. I would like to pay tribute to the natural beauty of Devon and beyond, which has been a perpetual inspiration to my poetry. Thanks, too, to my daughter, Miriam, for supplying the inspiration for 'Stealth', and for all her thoughtful comments on my poems. And, of course, for the opportunity to get some of my work properly out there at last – my grateful thanks for the support and enthusiastic efforts of Ronnie and Dawn!

*Catching Light* is Helen Boyles' first collection.

# CONTENTS

Earth Time, Devon ...................................................... 7

Trafalgar Woods ....................................................... 8

Otter ......................................................................... 9

Wicken Fen ............................................................. 10

Peregrine Watcher .................................................. 12

Stealth ..................................................................... 13

Welsh ....................................................................... 14

Dawlish Railway, Winter 2014 ............................. 15

Western Light .......................................................... 17

Swifts ....................................................................... 18

Laurebina Pass, Himalaya ..................................... 19

The Monk's Path ..................................................... 20

Bede of Jarrow ........................................................ 21

Courbet's Apples ..................................................... 23

Mrs. Radcliffe's Gothic ........................................... 24

William Blake, Engraver ........................................ 25

Dear Theo ................................................................ 26

Mary ........................................................................ 29

Casting Nets ........................................................... 31

Minsmere ................................................................ 33

Ancestral Voices ..................................................... 35

## Earth Time, Devon

Tunnel through Devonian time
in sunken lanes where red earth
packs the piled stone of old walls,
stains the fleece of grazing sheep,
deepening the warmth of hill
and banks of streams
sharp on their limestone beds.
Climb up from the deep combes
as time unfolds its strata,
leads you out into the sky
through mist and thinning grass,
wind-drifting light.
Return to emptied spaces
where the rivers rise,
birds spill their sad cadences,
see the frozen statements
of our molten origins
where heat of ancient turbulence
has sculpted history
in fists of granite dark against the sun.

## Trafalgar Woods

Dreadnought, Ajax, Orion, Thunderer:
*their syllables ring in the strokes*
*of the descending axe,*
*crack*
*and split the ancient silences.*
Achilles, Mars, Leviathan, Polyphemous:
*the gods of war possess the opened space.*
*Oak giants, felled with slicing light,*
*groan in a new birth*
*as* Royal Sovereign, Swiftsure
*and* Minotaur,
*navigate new winds and stars*
*to death and Victory.*

*Now commemorative plantings*
*resurrect their names as living masts,*
*push through the floors of hill and valley,*
*thrust aside the litter of the years until*
*they crowd the empty sky again*
*with branching rigging*
*hung with leaves and birds.*
*Now they stride the steady furrows,*
*repossess the land:*
Revenge, Defence, Defiance
Conqueror.

## Otter

Lose the weight of earth, the pull of stone
to free limbs in a liquid passage
underneath the trees,
leave the glare of day
to merge into the shadows
at the edge and deeper down,
ease boundaries between the real and dreamed.
Break the surface skin with wary eyes,
tense ears and nose then turn, dive,
Vanish, flick a beaded trail
in your receding wake.

This water-breathing skin
was sloughed long past
when we first tasted air
and clambered onto land,
the rudder muscle of a mermaid's tail
split into two, webbed pads shrunk
to hands and toes clawing dry surfaces.
Upright we faced the sun,
reached out our arms to distances,
defined our world with walls
and laid down stones for walking,
looked out on the sky through glass,
shut out the wind, the wet.

Yet water still dances in the deeps of our eyes,
shines and moves there,
threading memory and mind's meanderings,
and when we enter it in wild river swim
our otter spirit, otter self
uncurls from its secret holt,
spreads its limbs,
is born again.

## Wicken Fen

I held water,
stored secrets in the dark earth,
in trembling levels
caught the night stars.
Sky gazed down at me
and I shone back its light,
mirrored its changing faces
over and over.

Stands of sedge
and rushes' grey glint
spliced the horizontals,
intercepted space.
In rustling corridors
I played dry music
in the air's whorl,
muffled the sudden voices
of reed-haunting birds.

Hooves of cows and ponies
puddled water-softened ground.
People strode through me,
swam arms in my standing light,
gathered my crop
to slice and craft their homes.
Town-dwellers said their feet
were webbed
but we understood each other,
lived in wordless partnership.

Then came the engineers
with tools and ploughs
to reconstruct my space.
They drained my arteries,
stretched, stripped,

dried my colour to a sad blank.
The fen-folk disappeared
or shrank to engine operators
crawling on my drilled skin:
ploughed, sprayed,
levelled, emptied.
Beneath the weight
my heart beat slow and dull,
my silver voice
shrivelled to a husk.

But now the vision of the fen
dilates in a new light,
embraces a future
which reflects the sun again,
rings with the syllables
of the returning birds.
This time human visitors
step cautiously on raised boards,
protect themselves in waterproofs,
view me through the lens
of artificial eyes
from wooden refuges.
They take notes, scrutinize.

Will they ever wade
waist high through the mists again?
let the peat rust on their skin?
Will they flex their muscles
with the reed scythe,
gather once again
the fallen, diffused light
of harvest gods
and raise it up in praise
to an earth-old relationship?

### Peregrine Watcher
*(after j.a Baker's 'The Peregrine')*

Watch, follow,
and wait.
Watch until the watcher
becomes the watched,
until the follower
becomes the followed,
slow patience
to the stillness of a pool
silvered by the wind,
or a stirring grass,
or a waiting peregrine.
Camouflage with stubble
and with cloud,
or, newt-like, breathe
through your skin
the climate
and the colour of the day.
Wait
until a watchful presence
shades to invisibility,
enter
and lose the world again,
enter
and lose yourself.
Melt through the dividing line
of land and air,
revolve the distances,
flow and shift
from field to sea and sky,
dissolve into the deepest centre
of a falcon's eye.

## Stealth

She waits, emerges when the lights are dim,
fox-like, pads along the hidden ways,
breathes with the stirring secret life,
borrows eye-shine from its opened gaze.
Walls melt to bush and hill and flow
into the river's glide.
Bag on back and muffled in night's camouflage
she sneaks into the orchard in the valley bed
to graze and thieve a wasted crop.
Trees rustle with the waking owls
which loosen vowels in the
echo chamber of the waiting wood.
Shapeless and shape-shifting now
she stretches in the tree,
finds a crook, folds in its arms,
swings guiltless underneath the watching stars.
Shedding laws and boundaries,
blood rhythms swaying with blown calls
of night predators,
she spreads into the bark,
re-entering the spaces we have lost
or circumscribed
to reach and pluck those apples
gleaming in the moon's eye,
hug to herself the triumph
of this stolen prize.

## Welsh

Skirrid Fawr, Blaen Penant:
names speak land's history,
its foldings, fractures and collisions,
slow moulding into shapes
the mouth and mind can hold.
Ice scours the rock face,
chisels consonants in skid
and glitter ground to scree – Skirrid
tumbling to Fawr,
and in tear-scarred, seeping caves
a rush and slide
to vowel pools and openings.

Blaen Penant: crumbling walls
once raised and stacked
on turned land, now
a name alone, name
haunted by the moan
of air in blind stones
rubbed to friction by the winds
in breath of fricatives
and hiss of sibilance.
Labour carved its syllables,
the muscle haul and working hands
heaved rhythm, measuring
the steps and runs of speech,
landscape's swoops and arches
following its cadences.

## Dawlish Railway, Winter 2014

That long wet winter
we, our homes,
were punished by the elements,
beaten, battered,
inundated.
Water had crept up, swelled,
spilled
and flooded our defences,
in an instant
swept away our footings,
left us stranded above waves
hanging and afraid
as on a wild mountain bridge
slung between ravines.
We felt the pummelling
of wind,
the sough of air
in space,
heard the angry surge
of sea;
for a while we looked down,
around, above,
for explanation,
for solution.

Then townsfolk gathered efforts
to restore the south-west pride
of place in top five scenic rail routes,
claim the old delight
of breaking through the tunnel's gloom
to gasp of light,
glitter of sun on sea,
boats bright and bobbing
in the estuary,
birds stalking the tide's edge,

wet sand mirroring
their probing beaks.

We mend, restore,
buttress sand-soft cliffs,
work to keep the memory
at bay,
keep at bay the knowledge
of our power to abuse, impose,
ignore,
the power of nature
to retaliate.

## Western Light

Far Western isle translated by light.
Sky and sea light shafts and steals
from clouds and distances,
illuminates a script of stone,
of paths and waterways,
fingers
the letters of forgotten runes,
of winding field walls
built by famine- weakened hands.
Light resurrects their memories,
polishes
the surface of the waves
to molten glass,
sharpens
the edges of the hills,
brightens green,
deepens gold and indigo.
Light catches
the flight of birds,
windows, roofs of sleeping homes.
Light alters spaces,
shifts the relationship
of cliff to hill to sea,
opens through the veiling mist
new pathways into myth.
Then like a bird's wing
flashing into dark,
it vanishes
to reappear and startle us with hope,
blessing the holy stones
of ancient offerings,
kindling to vision curtained islands
poised on the silver rim
of a new world.

## Swifts

Later than most,
but sure as sun in spring
they burst onto our skies,
carve light with flashing wings.

High up, out of sight
we hear them scream and race,
chase flies; their high wild voices
sear our silences, devil's birds
beyond our safe perimeters.

If they fall, limp
shuffle of bone and feathers,
*apus apus*, instant prey.
Feet clasp brick or wood
to tend a nest tucked
in a crook of dark,
there clutch young
over resting weeks
until they flap and thrash
and feathered to flight
swoop off, take wing
to the pull of time, up, out,
to the call of distances.

Heart and wings beat their purpose
across continents,
windborne, airborne,
free of earth's drag.
We gaze at them with envy,
to the movement of memory,
watch them higher, further,
out of sight, suddenly heavy,
a sense of something gained,
something lost.

## Laurebina Pass, Himalaya

Mountain lodge floating on mist,
grey bulwark of the high pass,
labour's quarry, refuge for tired bones.
Struggling up, we perch on its platform,
order momo, wait.
A woman in Tibetan scarf and apron
spins cloud on her spool
then kneels and washes clothes,
kneading the rhythm of days
measured by hands, eyes, feet
in metal, cloth, stone.
A patient chiselling of hours
that hang, turn in the shifting light.
Time to carve syllables
and test them on the tongue,
weigh them in mind's silences.

Ringed by watching peaks,
wild spin of wind and snow,
thought curled in the whisper
of the ear's whorl untroubled
by the growl of storm, the rain's tattoo,
another sleeps and dreams of words.
He sees us, gestures;
wandering across, eyes smile, speak.
He is deaf, he mimes, but wants
to bridge space. He points to ear,
to mouth, our plates on the table.
'Food', he says; and turning
to the boy beside him: 'Brother'.
To a flapping shape above:
'Crow!' he exclaims,
and pointing higher, 'Sun!'

## The Monk's Path

On Easter Saturday
we went in search of ancient crosses
printing the steps of the Monk's Path
scattered over moor's
vast emptiness.
We followed their directions,
arms pointing East-West;
when we met them close up,
studied their scarred faces,
rubbed their broken arms.
They had been uprooted, robbed, scourged,
left for dead in tombs beneath grass
in rustling kitsvaaens of heather.
Seasons had grown over them;
they had grown blind with time.
Then feet had stumbled on them,
eyes had found,
hands had rescued them,
clamped and splinted broken limbs,
set them upright to bisect the sky,
shred drifting clouds,
sometimes a little skewed
but sturdy in their granite plinths.
Growing, hardening,
enduring;
inscribed with lichen, moss,
they hold out their arms,
link to each other over tramped miles,
point out and forward,
lead the eyes over the horizontals
to unclimbed heights
and distances.

## Bede of Jarrow

Mind bent on the waiting page,
hand moving quietly in careful cursive
latticing its white.
Body cloistered in stone
beaten by light and wind from marsh
and sea space
stretching to the edge of sight.

These stones were all he'd known,
confined, protected,
buttressed him from storm.
They served him, he served them
from youth to age
through interchange of mind,
of word,
embellishment of thought
in patient manuscript
relating lives and histories.
This was his cradle,
schoolroom, mentor's desk,
his company
and solitude.

Here, on Jarrow Slake,
outfacing greater tides,
he tuned into the voices
and the energies of cultures
from all compass points,
through faith's prism
traced their moulding
of the English race,
unlocked their treasures
in his meditative cell.
He watched sun rise
and set across the distances
through Frankish glass.

When he was dying he took gifts
from a casket
he had stowed away.
He had embraced simplicity
and poverty,
but he had linen napkins,
precious incense,
Indian peppercorns,
and these he gave
to those he loved.

Outside, sun blessed the sea.
Could he see the darkness
building up beneath,
hear the thunder of the surge,
see the longships
with their black prows
grind on shore to claim new ground,
their power
burst apart these still retreats
and torch the libraries,
the pride of Christendom?
Could he see them
spill English blood
and flood our arteries,
carve the runes of other stories
into ours,
their consonants into our tongues?

# Courbet's Apples

*(The French painter Gustav Courbet painted his 'Still Life with Apples and a Pomegranate' while in prison for his connection with the revolutionary Paris Commune of 1871)*

Still life: a stark space:
the dusk of his cell
smudges the angles of the walls
and seems to blur the contours of identity.
He tries to know himself
to feel his grounding
in his country's soil.
Walls can confine
but not obliterate, he thinks.
The orchards of his home
and his community
are planted in his mind,
and in the gloom they ripen into life.
In the shadows of his memory
their russets glow
and waking, he must grasp them.
Given paints, he finds the reds,
the autumn gold, stained greens
and conjures apples,
piles them in an earth brown dish
set on the peasant's working board,
balances their colours
with the dull gleam of a pewter jug
moulded to the user's hand.
He feels the fruit's coarse skin,
the windfall bruisings, knows
the beauty of the imperfections
in earth's rough, sweet offering.
Still Life: he gazes,
plucks them from the picture space,
and eats.

## Mrs. Radcliffe's Gothic

The firelight travels across her face
as she works, head bent, over her embroidery.
Its flicker quickens the colour of the threads.
Sometimes she tilts or shifts the complexion screen
to mask the blaze but more often likes to feel
its play of light and warmth over her mind
in the gliding silence of the evening house.

At invention's busy heart a picture grows
and gleams with stolen flame. Meticulous, deft-
fingered, the embroiderer weaves in its frame
a story's elements: a lonely chamber, dark
angle of the turret stair, pale face at the window,
winds the softer silks of shadow's mystery
to net the space beyond in a maze of passageways
unfolding caverns steeped in the chiaroscuro
of the dark sublime.

The needle's point directs us to the rim of vision,
tempts us with its glittering eye
to follow the threads further
but with an artist's final signature of confidence,
she smooths the rough edges,
tucks spare ends into a moral patterning
which returns us to the safety of the fireside seat,
the ticking heart of domesticity,
cold panes fastened on the silent dark.

Yet waiting there, beside the easy chair,
neatly bound and sorted in the work basket,
for the leisure of imagination's wandering,
the ravelled skeins of dreams.

## William Blake, Engraver

It is a humble space, but furnishes his needs,
enclosing bed and table workbench
and the graver's tool, window
framing the Thames' bar of gold.

Resting in the circle of Kate's stillness,
he graves and writes with steady passion,
lambent eyes, 'snub' nose and stubborn chin
transfigured by imagination's grace
into prophetic bard
encompassing the heavens, the abyss.

His mind sweeps visionary continents,
bends to the burin's point on chiselled plate,
rejects and wields compasses
to measure the perspective
of the spiritual eye, contain its force
within the bounding line of art.

Pinioned on joy,
he mounts with the praising lark,
knows the summits of light's freedom
 and the prison shades
of banishment.

Proud and humble he is
Los and Urizen,
creator and unmaker, wrath and pity
in the Tyger and the Lamb.
He is Orc's flaming energy
and patient discipline.
He is the fallen and redeemed,
he is the angel
on the ladder of the sun.

## Dear Theo

Dear Theo,

I am working hard, I am experimenting,
I am making studies of potato pickers.
*I must hold*
*and release the curve of back,*
*the scooping hand, the muscles' clench*
*in energy of line.*

I feel I have caught
the contours of this scene,
its scored and ancient face.
*Mind is grooved with field edge,*
*horizon's line*
*the body's lineaments*
*flow into space*
*and fill its springing emptiness.*

Dear Theo,

I am trying to reproduce the rhythm
of the sower's work,
the body's swing, the steady tread.
I show you in this sketch.
*I carve the landscape with his hunched shape*
*sweeping arm and open palm,*
*black slant of tree*
*scooped disc of moon.*

Dear Theo,

I strive to capture movement
in a stippled fleck and curling line
*Wind furrows the wheat*
*and lifts its gold to the lover's eye,*
*cloud blooms on the hill's back.*

Dear Theo,

Here is an open book:
you recognise the one .
I have applied a light tone on a dark ground.
*The page is blurred:*
*you may inscribe the sower's parable*

I have made a study of two empty chairs:      ·
the one is plain, a little rickety,
the other strong and elegant,
The sitter's things left on the seat
are waiting his return
*The floor is uneven*
*that is deliberate:*
*the blank chairs frame estrangement,*
*colours singe the painters' absences.*

Dear Theo,

I have been ill but I am gaining strength,
I have taken up my brush again
you will be glad to know.

*Others may lack heart,*
*you have humanity.*
*You have been kind; you hear,*
*but my pain is inarticulate.*
*The gaze of the world is veiled*
*with prejudice, indifference.*

*Now I see day*
*bleed the pigment of its last light.*
*Birds crowd the sky*
*to roost in the dark trees.*

*Truth burns*
*on the retina,*

*presses its vision in the heart*
*to burst its colours*
*in a final flowering,*
*final anointing of earth's womb,*
*earth's grave.*

Dear Theo,

*Forgive me,*
*Your loving brother, Vincent.*

## Mary

*(The last words of poet Seamus Heaney to his wife were 'Noli timere': 'do not be afraid).*

"Do not be afraid":
an angel, sudden
shiver of quills and light,
shining there before the trembling girl.
The stillness of hushed syllables:
"Do not be afraid".
Blessed among women,
you are a holy vessel,
channel of a future's hope
and more.
Guard your secret,
let it spill out when the time is right.

I am unworthy, weak,
and I confess, afraid,
but I shall nurse this message
and shall cup the spirit
in the chalice of my heart.

"Noli timere":
a dying poet to his Mary
at the bedside, head bowed,
fighting darkness, on the edge
of desolation. Be comforted:
Fear not.
Cherish what we know and have,
and what will come from this.
Violence clouds and fractures
families, communities,
can seem to smother hope
but cannot conquer.
Earth seethes with memories
and new awakenings.

Forgiveness heals,
ordinary love endures.
Poetry will honour this,
will honour you:
Remember this
and store it in the chalice of your heart.

I will.

The angel left.

A shining space.

## Casting Nets

Last light flickers,
dies on the water's skin,
deepens to ink.
Slowly you cast moorings loose,
push from the edge
and drift out on the flood;
your nets unravel,
spread and billow in the black.

You trawl the deeps of the long night
for nourishment.
The vessel creaks, the water sighs,
clouds glide by unseen

You strain sight for the glint of scales below,
the flash of fluid motion in the clouded
stillness of the underworld.
All dark.
Time sinks,
sits heavy on the prow;
limp and light, nets
hang in the void.

Weeds sway and mass, but threaten to engulf,
offer no hiding place this time,
no refuge for the timid opportunity.
Heart searches the drowned caves
but finds no voice or pulse,
no resonance.

Breath, air lightens gradually
to dawn as shadows shift,
outlines wavering,
rocks silvering.

Then you detect a presence,
cowled, mysterious,
the far side of the shore
of consciousness:
a figure standing, watching there.
Clear and strong a voice calls through the mist,
drops into the hollow of the silence
like a bell.

*Cast your nets the other side.*
*Cast them.*
*Trust, and cast them now.*

Other hands and strength join yours
to drop the net again the other side
and then together haul up
gleaming shoals
that thrash and wriggle in the straining mesh.

Is this reality? A dream that will dissolve
as the sun mounts,
the colours dull to pewter, disappear?
We have to hope,
need to believe: the heart insists.

And now as we glance out to the unveiling shore,
we see the figure stoop, prepare a fire of sticks,
kneel to blow flame.
Hands cup the light.
There he awaits the treasure landed as an offering
to be shared, consumed,
as darkness lifts.

## Minsmere

Light on reed
beckons the eye
in glance and shimmer
on the marsh's face,
translates to shapes
which flicker out of sight,
melt into the shade of wood or sedge.
We watch from above
in spy-hides by the meres;
they watch within the grasses
or the leaves,
eyes meeting
or avoiding scrutiny.

Floss of goat willow,
fleece of sedge
drifts and catches sun,
white glint on a martin's back,
a swallow's throat,
cap of a harrier
hanging in the updraft
high in space.
Eyes meet eyes:
upward glances bright and quick
beneath the shaking stems,
steady downward gaze fine-
chiselled to an arrow's shaft
trained on the crouched and nervous shape
that wills invisibility.
Stalking reed-bed hunter
stretches into verticals,
narrows into stripes and ripples,
stoops, bends,
pounces, swallows,
waits.

Sounds tease ears
bent on the stillness:
flight-screams tearing overhead,
twitch and rattles in the sedge,
a cuckoo's floating monody,
the bittern boom,
low, primal,
resonating across distances.
All is quick and sharp
and secret:
we prime and lengthen telescopes,
adjust binoculars,
hang on the edges
of this private busyness,
startled with sightings
as the rare and delicate celebrities
flash into vision for applause,
dazzle with glamour,
meet in patternings
of dance and song,
tease us with hope and possibility
to vanish on a wind and breath
into the wings.
There they fold
the knowledge of their movements
and their lines,
unravelling their hidden narratives.

## Ancestral Voices

Each night sleep loosens thought's mooring,
casts the mind adrift
in the warped cask of dreams,
onto the stealthy flood of memory.
From the trees' mass owl calls
rise like smoke shapes from the dusk,
blow their spell in stillness feathered
with forgotten sounds that drift
from the abandoned caves, stir light
in strewn embers from the distant day.
They float us to the forest edge,
where, through its shifting screen
we glimpse fire blaze again, tools gleam,
mouths shape the syllables of speech,
move in command, or love.

Sometimes a ragged wind
buffets the mind's journey,
beats the torn sail in the face,
troubles with strange currents,
unexpected rocks,
till coming back along the night dark lane,
the eye is guided by a moving light,
the ear arrested by the hushed rush
of a swan's smooth flight
that, like a greeting from lost gods,
unfolds calm in turbulence,
carves a steady furrow
through imagination's wandering,
ploughs the swan-road
back to the ancestral hearth.

Indigo Dreams Publishing Ltd
24, Forest Houses
Cookworthy Moor
Halwill
Beaworthy
Devon
EX21 5UU
www.indigodreams.co.uk